ASPECTS OF BRITISH HISTORY BEYOND 1066

THE CHANGING POWER OF THE
BRITISH MONARCHY

Ben Hubbard

raintree
a Capstone company — publishers for children

Raintree is an imprint of Capstone Global Library Limited, a company incorporated in England and Wales having its registered office at 264 Banbury Road, Oxford, OX2 7DY – Registered company number: 6695582

www.raintree.co.uk
myorders@raintree.co.uk

Edited by Helen Cox Cannons
Designed by Philippa Jenkins
Original illustrations © Capstone Global Library Limited 2018
Picture research by Svetlana Zhurkin
Production by Steve Walker
Originated by Capstone Global Library Limited
Printed and bound in China

ISBN 978 1 4747 4136 1
21 20 19 18 17
10 9 8 7 6 5 4 3 2 1

British Library Cataloguing in Publication Data
A full catalogue record for this book is available from the British Library.

Acknowledgements
We would like to thank the following for permission to reproduce photographs: Alamy: Heritage Image Partnership, 6, Lebrecht Music and Arts Photo Library, 21, Pictorial Press, 20; Bridgeman Images: Look and Learn/Private Collection/Elizabeth I (1533-1603) The Warrior Queen (gouache on paper), Doughty, C.L. (1913-85), 13; Getty Images: Heritage Images/Fine Art Images, 19, Popperfoto, 24; iStockphoto: duncan1890, cover, 1, 8, 10, Tony Baggett, 16, traveler1116, 9; Mary Evans Picture Library, 22; Newscom: akg-images/Sotheby's, 17, David Cole, 23, Heritage Images/Ann Ronan Picture Library, 11, Heritage Images/The Print Collector, 15, 18, Le Pictorium/Active Museum, 14, Photoshot, 26, 27, Photoshot/LFI/John Shelley Collection, 25, World History Archive, 5; Shutterstock: Andreas Berheide, cover and throughout (flag), Everett Historical, 12, Ivan Ponomarev, 30, Valery Egorov, 7, Viacheslav Rashevskyi, 9 and throught (crown).

We would like to thank Dr Lesley Robinson for her invaluable help in the preparation of this book.

Every effort has been made to contact copyright holders of material reproduced in this book. Any omissions will be rectified in subsequent printings if notice is given to the publisher.

All the internet addresses (URLs) given in this book were valid at the time of going to press. However, due to the dynamic nature of the internet, some addresses may have changed, or sites may have changed or ceased to exist since publication. While the author and publisher regret any inconvenience this may cause readers, no responsibility for any such changes can be accepted by either the author or the publisher.

CONTENTS

Some words in this book appear in bold, **like this**. You can find out what they mean by looking in the glossary.

INTRODUCTION

In 1066, during Anglo-Saxon times, a Norman duke called William the Conqueror came over from northern France and **invaded** England. The king, Harold, met William in battle near Hastings, East Sussex. Harold and his Anglo-Saxon men were outnumbered but they fought bravely against William's army. However, all was lost when Harold was killed in battle. England now belonged to William and the Normans.

EARLY INVADERS

William was not the first foreigner to invade England. Before William, the Anglo-Saxons had invaded Britain, during the 5th century. Before that, the Romans had invaded. Early Anglo-Saxon kings ruled over five main regions of England. From the time of William, England – and later Britain – would be ruled over by one **monarch**.

CHANGING ROLE OF THE MONARCHY

The first English monarchs ruled as **absolute monarchs**. They could demand **taxes** at any time, make people go to war and punish them with death if they disobeyed them. Over the centuries, power struggles between the ordinary people and the monarch have at times caused unrest and violence. The British monarch's role slowly changed. Now a British monarch is king or queen in name only. This is the story of how that happened.

INHERITING THE THRONE

A person becomes king or queen by being born into the British royal family. For centuries, the monarch's eldest male child was the first in line to the throne. This meant it was important for a monarch to produce a male **heir**. Before the 16th century, when Mary I and Elizabeth I reigned, the idea of a female inheriting the throne was simply unthinkable. After this, a daughter could become queen if there were no surviving sons. In 2015 the law changed. Now it is the monarch's eldest child – male or female – who is heir to the throne.

The section of the Bayeux Tapestry showing Harold with an arrow in his eye

THE NORMANS

On Christmas Day, 1066, William crowned himself King William I of England. The Anglo-Saxons hated their new king and formed **uprisings** against him. However, William ruled with an iron fist. He sent his soldiers to crush the uprisings. Thousands of Anglo-Saxons were killed as a result.

THE FEUDAL SYSTEM

Next, William took away lands belonging to the Anglo-Saxons. He then gave the lands to his Norman **barons** (nobles). In return, the barons had to swear their loyalty to William and collect **taxes** from the local people. They also had to provide men for William's army. This way of managing the country was called the **feudal system**. At the top of the system, William ruled as an **absolute monarch**.

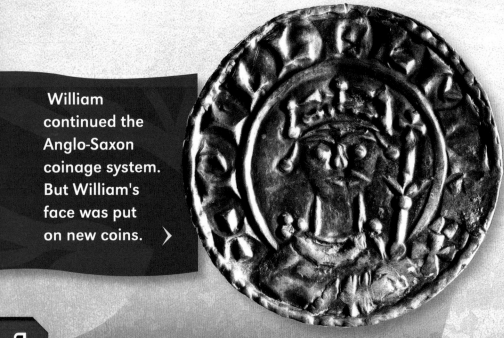

William continued the Anglo-Saxon coinage system. But William's face was put on new coins. ❯

CASTLES AND CHURCHES

William and his barons built large stone castles to show off their power and control their lands. Knights and soldiers living at the castles could easily ride out to crush local uprisings. Ordinary people travelled to their baron's castle to pay tax. People also met to worship at churches. The national religion at that time was **Catholicism**.

Rochester Castle was one of the castles built during Norman times. It is still standing today.

THE DOMESDAY BOOK

To work out how much tax each person would pay, William sent his men all around England. They recorded who owned what and how much of everything there was, including houses, animals and land. They wrote down these facts in a huge book, called the Domesday Book. It is Britain's oldest surviving public record and is today stored in the National Archives in London.

THE PLANTAGENETS

PLANTAGENET FAMILY TREE BY RULING DATES:
HENRY II (1154–1189) → RICHARD I (1189–1199) → JOHN (1199–1216)
→ HENRY III (1216–1272)

A line of rulers from the same family is known as a **dynasty**. The Plantagenets were a dynasty. They ruled England after the Normans. Henry II was the first Plantagenet king. He ruled over an empire that covered England, France, Ireland, Wales and Scotland. Henry's son, Richard I, was known as "the Lionheart". After Richard died abroad, his brother John became king.

THE "BAD" KING

John was an unpopular ruler. Called "Bad King John", he lost his father's French lands, raised **taxes** and argued with the **Pope** (the head of the **Catholic** church). The Pope then banned all English church services. This made John's **barons** angry.

> Richard "the Lionheart" spent most of his reign fighting abroad.

THE MAGNA CARTA

In 1215, the English barons raised an army against John. They made John sign a document called the Magna Carta. This limited the power of the king and gave all people basic **rights**. John could no longer raise taxes, tell the church what to do or ignore people's wishes. It also meant John could no longer rule as an **absolute monarch**.

King John, signing the Magna Carta

Regal fact

King John had a bath every three weeks. This was considered very often at this time!

THE BIRTH OF PARLIAMENT

Simon de Montfort was a rebel baron. He wanted the king to have less power over his people. In 1264, Simon imprisoned King Henry III (King John's son) and called a special **parliament**. This was made up of nobles, **clergy**, knights and ordinary people. It was the first time the different classes had met to discuss matters and is considered an early version of today's parliament.

THE TUDORS

The next powerful **dynasty** to rule over England was the Tudors. They took control of the country after a series of wars between 1455 and 1485. These wars became known as the Wars of the Roses. The first Tudor king was Henry VII. Henry became rich by raising **taxes** and encouraging trade. He also took power away from his nobles by banning their private armies. With the nobles weakened, Henry was a powerful king.

Henry VIII

HENRY VIII AND THE CHURCH

Henry VIII was Henry VII's son. He was used to getting his own way. When his wife Catherine of Aragon could not give him a son, Henry asked the **Pope** to divorce them. Henry hoped to get divorced so he could marry Anne Boleyn. When the Pope said no, Henry was furious. He asked his **parliament** to ban the **Catholic** church. He then turned England into a **Protestant** country.

POWER THROUGH PARLIAMENT

Henry asked parliament to close every Catholic **monastery** in England. Henry was sneaky: by doing things through parliament nobody could claim he was an **absolute monarch**. However, the members of parliament often only agreed with Henry because they were scared. Next, Henry stole the monasteries' treasures to start a war with France. When the war failed, England was left nearly bankrupt (having no money).

⌃ Anne Boleyn was Henry VIII's second wife and the first English queen ever to be executed.

Regal fact

Henry employed a servant called "the groom of the stool" to help him on the toilet!

HENRY'S SIX WIVES

Henry married six times. Henry divorced two wives and had two others **beheaded**. Jane Seymour, Henry's third wife, was the only wife to bear Henry a male **heir** – the future Edward VI. She died 12 days later. His sixth wife outlived him.

"BLOODY MARY"

After Henry VIII's death, his longed-for son, Edward VI, became king. But at the age of only 15, Edward died after a period of illness. In 1553, Edward's half-sister Mary I became queen. She brought back **Catholicism** as the national religion. Mary had hundreds of Protestants burned at the stake. For this, she later became known as "Bloody Mary".

A NEW QUEEN

After Mary's death, her half-sister Elizabeth became queen, as Elizabeth I. Elizabeth wanted to make England a Protestant country again. Elizabeth was a clever **monarch**. She kept some aspects of Catholicism to keep everyone happy. She said everything she did was for her subjects and used her charm to control parliament. However, as queen, Elizabeth always had the final say.

This painting shows Elizabeth being carried by courtiers. >

Regal fact

Elizabeth chose not to marry. She instead claimed that she was married to the kingdom of England.

When the Spanish Armada sailed into the English Channel, Elizabeth I made a powerful speech to rally her troops.

THE "GOLDEN ERA"

Under Elizabeth, England enjoyed a "golden era" of foreign trade and exploration. Elizabeth ruled like an absolute monarch but she died a much-loved queen. She showed everyone that she was a more successful ruler than many of the kings who had gone before her.

QUEEN AND COMMANDER

In 1588, King Phillip of Spain wanted to restore Catholicism to England. He sent his Spanish Armada (fleet of warships) to invade. Elizabeth rallied her navy by saying, "I know I have but the body of a weak and feeble woman, but I have the heart and stomach of a king." After the English defeated the Spanish, no one doubted Elizabeth's abilities as a queen in wartime.

THE STUARTS

STUART FAMILY TREE BY RULING DATES:
JAMES I (1603–1625) → CHARLES I (1625–1649) → CHARLES II (1660–1685)
→ JAMES II (1685–1688)

In 1603, Elizabeth I died without an **heir**. A Scottish royal **dynasty** called the Stuarts **succeeded** Elizabeth and the Tudors. The new king, James VI of Scotland, also became King James I of England. This united both nations. James believed in the "divine right of kings". This means that he believed the **monarch** had been chosen by God and should not be questioned. As a result, James often clashed with **parliament** when it disagreed with him.

James I of England
and VI of Scotland

CHARLES RAISES TAXES

When James I died, his son Charles became king, as Charles I. Charles also believed in the divine right of kings. Charles **disbanded** parliament several times, and at one stage he ruled without parliament for 11 years. During this time, Charles raised **taxes** and became very unpopular. When Charles finally allowed parliament to meet he tried to arrest five of its members for **treason**. Civil war broke out.

THE ENGLISH CIVIL WAR

The English Civil War divided the country. On one side were King Charles' supporters. They were known as the Cavaliers. Opposing the Cavaliers were the Roundheads. The Roundheads were led by Oliver Cromwell (1599–1658), a **member of parliament** (MP). King Charles was defeated at the 1645 Battle of Naseby and later imprisoned. He was sentenced to death for treason.

AN UNCERTAIN FUTURE

Because he believed in the "divine right of kings", Charles I argued that no court on Earth could judge a king – only God could do that. Therefore, on 30 January 1649, when Charles was **beheaded**, it showed that parliament had more power than the king. Without a monarch, nobody knew what would come next.

This painting shows Charles I being led to his execution in 1649.

REPUBLIC NATION

After Charles' execution, parliament decided that the country should become a **republic** instead of having a monarchy. This meant that the parliament would rule, with Oliver Cromwell at its head. Cromwell believed a ruler should have the public's approval and not just rule because they were born into that position.

CROMWELL'S CROWN

Not everyone wanted the monarchy to end. Charles I's son, also named Charles, had fled to France. Now he raised an army to try and claim the throne. However, in 1651, Charles's army was defeated by Cromwell's army at the Battle of Worcester. Parliament offered to make Cromwell king but he called himself Lord Protector instead. Cromwell then formed a new type of **government** called the **Protectorate**. In some ways Cromwell ruled like a king – he dismissed the parliament when it disagreed with him.

This illustration shows Cromwell (centre) dismissing parliament.

CROMWELL'S SON

When Cromwell died in 1658, his son Richard became Lord Protector. But Richard was a weak ruler and resigned (gave up) after a year. Many people then wondered if **abolishing** the monarchy had been a good idea. In 1660, the parliament invited Charles II to return to England and become king.

CHARLES RETURNS AS KING

At first, the people welcomed Charles II with open arms. Then they became suspicious when he argued with parliament about religion. After his brother James (later James II) became a **Catholic**, people were afraid that Charles would restore **Catholicism** to England. When parliament tried to make a law that no Catholic could become king, Charles disbanded it.

Charles II

A NEW KING

In 1685, **parliament's** worst fears came true. Charles II died and was **succeeded** by his **Catholic** brother, James, who became James II. James II promised parliament that he did not want to restore **Catholicism** as a national faith. However, in 1688, James's wife Mary gave birth to a son. This alarmed parliament – now there was a Catholic **heir** to the throne.

ORANGE OVERTHROW

Members of the parliament asked the Dutch king, William of Orange, to overthrow James II. William agreed to "rescue the religion and the nation" and **invaded** England. Fearing for his safety, James fled to France. On 11 April 1689, William III and his wife Mary II were crowned king and queen at Westminster Abbey. This became known as the Glorious Revolution.

This illustration shows parliament offering the crown to William and Mary. ›

A CONSTITUTIONAL MONARCHY

In 1689, a very important event happened in parliament that changed the relationship between the monarchy and **government**. William and Mary signed parliament's Bill of **Rights**. The bill greatly limited the powers of a British **monarch**. Monarchs were no longer allowed to raise **taxes**, gather an army or pass laws without parliament's approval. This arrangement is known as a **constitutional monarchy** and it is still in place today.

QUEEN ANNE

Because William and Mary had no **heirs**, the parliament chose Mary's sister Anne as the next queen. In 1707, the Act of Union passed through parliament. This Act put the English parliament in Westminster in charge of England, Scotland and Wales under the new name of the "United Kingdom of Great Britain". Queen Anne therefore became the first monarch to rule over Great Britain.

Queen Anne

Regal fact

Anne became pregnant 18 times to her husband, Prince George of Denmark, but none of her children survived. She died without an heir.

THE HANOVERIANS

HANOVERIAN FAMILY TREE BY RULING DATES:
GEORGE I (1714−1727) → GEORGE II (1727−1760) → GEORGE III (1760−1820)
→ GEORGE IV (1820−1830) → WILLIAM IV (1830−1837) → VICTORIA (1837−1901)

After Queen Anne died, the only people with a claim to the English throne were **Catholic**. However, **parliament's** 1701 Act of Settlement stated that no Catholic could ever again be a British **monarch**. Parliament therefore had to choose a new **Protestant dynasty** to rule. It chose the German Hanoverians. This was because Sophia of Hanover was James I's granddaughter and also a Protestant. However, there was a problem. The first Hanoverian king, who was Sophia's son George I, could barely speak English.

THE JACOBITE UPRISING

Some Catholics called **Jacobites** believed that James II's son, James Stuart, should be king. Known as the "Old Pretender", James Stuart staged an **uprising** in 1715. However, he was easily defeated by the Hanoverian army. James's son, Charles Edward Stuart, tried again in 1745 after raising an army in Scotland. However, this uprising by the man named the "Young Pretender" also failed.

Charles Edward Stuart was also known as "Bonnie Prince Charlie".

ROBERT WALPOLE

George's poor English and lack of knowledge about the British **government** made him unpopular. There was no point in George going to parliamentary meetings when he couldn't understand what was being said. Instead, George asked **member of parliament** (MP) Robert Walpole (1676–1745) to go. This effectively made Robert Walpole the first Prime Minister of Britain.

THE POWER OF PARLIAMENT

Having a prime minister led to a shift in power between parliament and the king or queen. At first, monarchs chose their prime ministers, but after the reign of King George III this also changed. Prime ministers were then elected into that position. This meant that talented people could be in positions of power rather than being born into them.

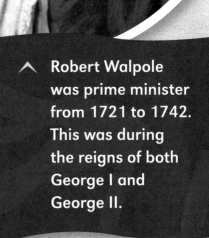

 Robert Walpole was prime minister from 1721 to 1742. This was during the reigns of both George I and George II.

A YOUNG QUEEN

Queen Victoria came to the throne at 18 years of age. She ruled for 63 years. By the time of her death, Britain had become a major global power with a huge British Empire. However, Victoria herself had less political power than any monarch who had come before her.

SHAPING THE ROLE

During Victoria's reign, new voting systems gave parliament more power and the monarchy less. One writer said the monarch's only remaining power was "the **right** to be consulted, the right to encourage and the right to warn." Some people wondered why there was a monarchy at all and called for it to be **abolished**. It was up to Victoria and her husband Albert to shape a new role for the royal family.

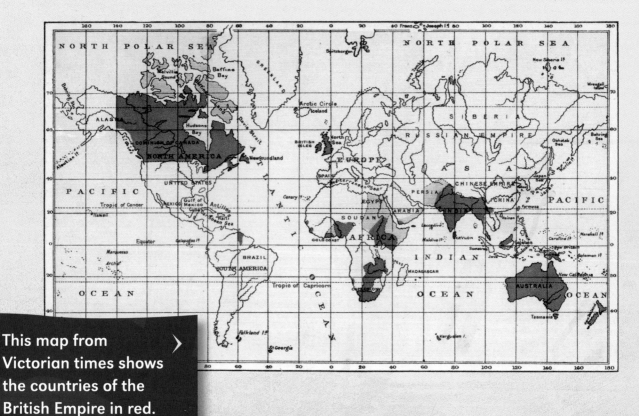

This map from Victorian times shows the countries of the British Empire in red.

THE UNITING QUEEN

Although she had little political power, Victoria became a great symbolic figure as queen. Her face could be seen on stamps and coins throughout the empire and she had many places in Australia, Africa and Canada named after her. In this way, Victoria created the new role of the modern monarch: a figurehead that unites people in royal pride.

↑ Queen Victoria in 1897, at her Diamond Jubilee (60 years of ruling)

SHORT BUT STRONG

Victoria and Albert showed that the monarchy was important by supporting charities, opening museums and attending events around the country. Although Victoria was short, she had a big personality and strong values. She and Albert tried to live as normally as possible and the public looked up to them and their children as the ideal Victorian family.

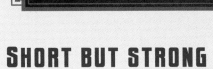

Regal fact

When Victoria learned at 10 years old that she would become queen, she said, "I will be good".

THE WINDSORS

WINDSOR FAMILY TREE BY RULING DATES
GEORGE V (1910–1936) → EDWARD VIII (JAN–DEC 1936) → GEORGE VI (1936–1952) → ELIZABETH (1952–)

Replacing the Hanoverian royal family were the **monarchs** of today: the Windsors. Originally called the German name Saxe-Coburg-Gotha, the Windsors changed their name to avoid anti-German feeling in World War I (1914–1918). The Windsor monarchs have lived through many changes: two world wars, the end of the British Empire and the dawn of an age of **mass media**.

Edward VIII and Wallis Simpson

24

PRINCESS DIANA

Media interest in the royal family, particularly in Diana, Princess of Wales, reached its peak in the 1990s. Photographers could sell their pictures for large sums of money to newspapers. Some photographers were chasing Princess Diana in 1997 when her car crashed and she was killed. The royal relationship with the media changed after that.

PUBLIC LIFE

The Windsors have only ever held a ceremonial role as monarchs. They have always lived in the public eye. Newspapers, radio, television and the internet have helped the Windsors connect with their subjects. But this has also meant their royal **scandals** have been widely reported.

ROYAL SCANDALS

In 1936, King Edward VIII created a scandal when he abdicated (gave up the throne) to marry an American woman called Wallis Simpson. This was because **parliament** decided it would be wrong for the monarch to marry a divorced woman.

Edward's brother, George VI, then became king. He needed to renew public faith in the monarchy. He did this by becoming a symbol of bravery during World War II (1939–1945). George, his wife Queen Elizabeth and their daughters, princesses Elizabeth and Margaret, stayed in London throughout the war, even after Buckingham Palace was bombed.

THE YOUNG QUEEN

Queen Elizabeth II inherited the throne from her father, George VI. She was crowned on 2 June 1953 at 27 years of age. From an early age, Elizabeth took her royal role seriously. During her reign she has tried to keep the monarchy up to date with the modern world.

NASTY NINETIES

Elizabeth's reign has not been without trouble. In the 1990s, three of Elizabeth's children divorced, fire swept through Windsor Castle and Princess Diana died. The royal family were also criticized in the newspapers for costing the UK too much money. Many called for the monarchy to be **abolished**. Despite this, Elizabeth is still very popular, especially since her Diamond Jubilee in 2012.

Elizabeth II has ruled for longer than any other monarch in British history.

MODERN DUTIES

Under today's **constitutional monarchy**, the Queen is the head of state but she performs only a ceremonial role. Her duties include attending formal events, holding receptions for world leaders and supporting over 600 charities. Although Elizabeth has no political power, she meets with the Prime Minister weekly to talk about political matters.

WHO WILL BE NEXT?

Elizabeth will be **succeeded** by her son Charles, who will become Charles III. His son, Prince William, will be king after him. It has always been a royal duty to produce an **heir** and William has two children, George and Charlotte. As a modern royal, William does his best to appear to his public as a sensitive and serious monarch in waiting.

Regal fact

Elizabeth II has owned more than 30 corgi dogs during her reign.

Prince William and his wife Catherine perform many royal duties. This photo of them with George and Charlotte was taken on their 2016 royal tour of Canada.

TIMELINE

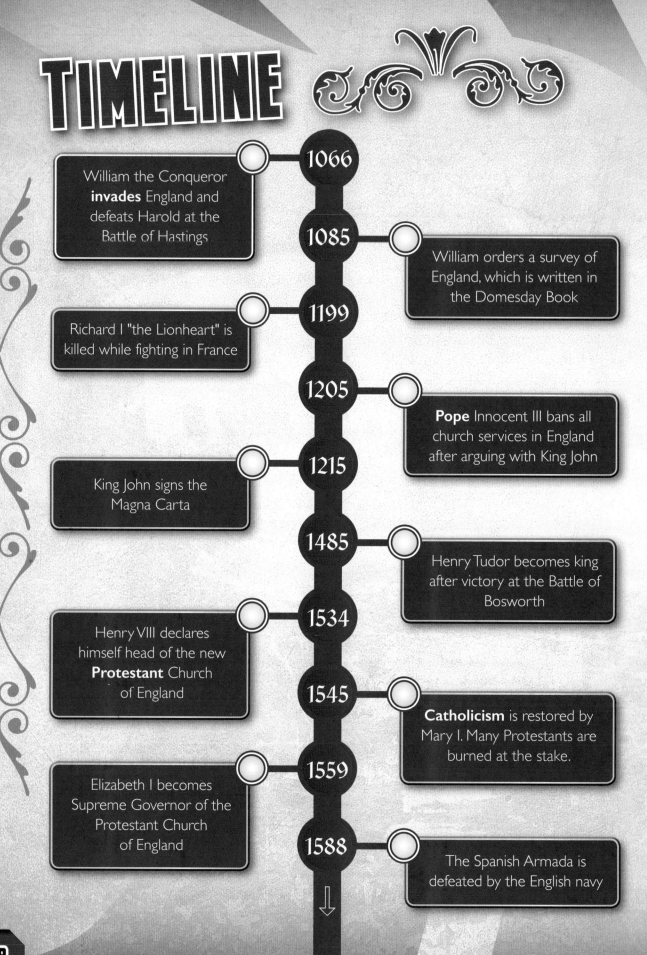

1066
William the Conqueror **invades** England and defeats Harold at the Battle of Hastings

1085
William orders a survey of England, which is written in the Domesday Book

1199
Richard I "the Lionheart" is killed while fighting in France

1205
Pope Innocent III bans all church services in England after arguing with King John

1215
King John signs the Magna Carta

1485
Henry Tudor becomes king after victory at the Battle of Bosworth

1534
Henry VIII declares himself head of the new **Protestant** Church of England

1545
Catholicism is restored by Mary I. Many Protestants are burned at the stake.

1559
Elizabeth I becomes Supreme Governor of the Protestant Church of England

1588
The Spanish Armada is defeated by the English navy

1625

Charles I **disbands parliament** for the first time

1649

Execution of Charles I. The monarchy is **abolished**. England becomes a **republic**.

1653

Oliver Cromwell becomes Lord Protector of England

1660

The monarchy is restored under Charles II

1707

Act of Union leads to the formation of Great Britain

1840

Queen Victoria marries Albert of Saxe-Coburg-Gotha

1901

Death of Queen Victoria

1936

Edward VIII shocks the people by stepping down as king. George VI becomes king instead.

1953

Elizabeth II has her coronation at Westminster Abbey

1969

Elizabeth II allows BBC to film documentary about private lives of royal family

2015

Elizabeth II becomes the longest-reigning British **monarch**

GLOSSARY

abolish stop or put an end to

absolute monarch king or queen with complete power over a country and its people

baron noble who rules over land given by the monarch

behead chop a person's head off

Catholic member of the Roman Catholic church ruled by the Pope in Rome

Catholicism beliefs of the Catholic church

constitutional monarchy government with the monarch as head of state but whose parliament runs the country

clergy ministers or priests of the church

disband let go, or send away

feudal system system where nobles hold land for a monarch in return for taxes and soldiers

government group of people elected to control and organize a country

heir person who is next in line to the throne

invade enter another country by force to try and take it over

Jacobite supporter of the claim to the throne by James II and the Stuarts

mass media worldwide communication by radio, television, newspapers, films and the internet

member of parliament (MP) person elected by voters to represent them in parliament

monarch hereditary ruler, such as a queen or king

monastery building lived in by Catholic monks

parliament group of elected members who make up a government

Pope head of the Catholic church

Protestant member of the Christian Church which separated from the Roman Catholic church during the 16th century

republic state ruled over by the people and their elected government instead of a monarch

rights certain basic privileges that people are entitled to, such as legal or human rights

scandal anger or outrage caused when people find out about something

succeed take over a position from someone

tax money paid by citizens to the government to help run the country

treason disloyal behaviour towards, or crime against, the king or queen

uprising act of protest or rebellion

FIND OUT MORE

BOOKS

All About Henry VIII (Fusion: History), Anna Claybourne, (Raintree, 2015)

Elizabeth I and Queen Victoria (Comparing People from the Past), Nick Hunter, (Raintree, 2016)

Henry's Heads: Henry VIII (History), Anna Claybourne, (Raintree, 2015)

WEBSITES

http://www.bbc.co.uk/schools/primaryhistory/famouspeople/famous_monarchs/
This interactive website from the BBC has many facts about British kings and queens, including Elizabeth I and Queen Victoria.

https://www.royal.uk
The official website for the royal family, with links to who they are and what they do.

http://www.theschoolrun.com/homework-help/queen-elizabeth-ii
A website for children about the royal family, including video clips of Queen Elizabeth II as a girl, and activities.

http://www.activityvillage.co.uk/british-royal-family
A fun website with British Royal Family activities, puzzles and colouring pages.

INDEX